D0588400

Lock Up Your Sons!

Ribald Rhymes Number Nine

Lock Up Your Sons!

Ribald Rhymes Number Nine

Clive Murphy

Brick Lane Books
London

Published in 2014 by Brick Lane Books
132 Brick Lane, London E1 6RU
Tel: +44 (020) 7247 6626
Website: www.clivemurphy.org

ISBN: 978-0-9541563-7-4

All rights reserved

Copyright © Clive Murphy 2014

British Library Cataloguing in Publication Data
A catalogue record for this book is
available from The British Library

Cover illustration by Quark
Cover photograph by Gerry King

Printed in Great Britain by
CPI Group (UK) Ltd., Croydon CR0 4YY

Headings and text set in
Book Antigua

Distributed by the Publisher

By the same author

Verse:

SOUR GRAPES (illustrated)
CAVE CANEM
ORTS AND ALL
LUST AND MALICE
SODOMY IS NOT ENOUGH!
HEAVENLY BLUE
GAY ABANDON
ON PLEASURE BENT (Illustrated)``

Fiction:

SUMMER OVERTURES
FREEDOM FOR MR MILDEW
NIGEL SOMEONE

Recorded autobiographies:

THE GOOD DEEDS OF A GOOD WOMAN
The memoirs of an East End hostel-dweller
BEATRICE ALI

BORN TO SING
The memoirs of an East End mantle presser
ALEXANDER HARTOG

FOUR ACRES AND A DONKEY
The memoirs of a lavatory attendant
S.A.B. ROGERS

LOVE, DEARS!
The memoirs of a former chorus girl
MARJORIE GRAHAM
(Also published as 'Up in Lights')

OIKY
The memoirs of a pigman
LEN MILLS

AT THE DOG IN DULWICH
The memoirs of a poet
PATRICIA DOUBELL

A STRANGER IN GLOUCESTER
The memoirs of an Austrian in England
MRS FALGE-WAHL

A FUNNY OLD QUIST
The memoirs of a gamekeeper
EVAN ROGERS

DODO
The memoirs of a left-wing socialite
DODO LEES

ENDSLEIGH
The memoirs of a river-keeper
HORACE ADAMS

In preparation:

APRIL FOOL
The memoirs of a former prep school headmaster
EVAN HOPE-GILL

ANGEL OF THE SHADOWS
The memoirs of a cat lady
JOAN LAUDER

TEARAWAY
The memoirs of a transsexual
ANGELLA-DEE SHERRIFFE, formerly David A. Sherriff

and

A LUDICROUS OLD AGE – DIARIES OF CLIVE MURPHY

SELIM, SLOW LEARNER – A LIFE OBSERVED

OF CLIVE MURPHY'S SERIES OF RECORDED AUTOBIOGRAPHIES:
'Marvellous work, full of vitality, humour, courage and street
sadness.'   *Patrick Garland*

As midwife rather than ghost, Clive Murphy has delivered an
eloquent child whose chatter has a way of slipping into revelation.'
                                                   Ronald Blythe

OF HIS NOVELS:

Freedom for Mr. Mildew and Nigel Someone

'Mr. Murphy's comedy has a delicately lethal edge to it . . . .
Obsession, obsessively recorded, is irresistible.'
                                              Victoria Glendinning

'His writing is sparse and witty, and he has the rare ability to be
both comic and compassionate.'   *British Book News*

'The reader is introduced to some facts about pain . . . .

If it doesn't choke on its own bile Clive Murphy's talent will
hopefully grow into something big.'   *Irish Independent, 1975*

'A chill pair of extended short stories.'   *Irish Press*

'It's a long time since I came across a new writer so perfectly
equipped to cut down the high-minded.'
                             Pearse Hutchinson on Radio Eireann

Summer Overtures

'The themes of homosexual and
heterosexual adventures move
along with the verve and colour of
a catherine-wheel spinning out of
control.'   *The Listener*

'Animated, gifted.'   *The Times*

'The characters are quite effortlessly
eccentric.'   *The Sunday Times*

'A very enjoyable and
accomplished black comedy.'
                    The Glasgow Herald

'Sulphurous sketches of life
at several different levels
of decay - personal, social,
even in a sense political.'
          Adam International Review

'It makes angelic use of
words (and sentences and
paragraphs). It is lucid,
cool, sly and inventive; may
well be required reading,
having become a classic.'
    Brigid Brophy in the Spectator

Special thanks are due to Wendy French
for formatting and layout.

For
Stefan Dickers

A man gets tired of the same man all the time.

Adapted from Sidney Bechet's 'Preachin' Blues'

We have no taste: we are artists.

Gilbert and George

CONTENTS

Promiscuity 1

Paranoia 1

Housemaster's Pep Talk to recent Admission 2

Obdurate Feminist on a Royal Firstborn 2

Dinner-Party Spat 3

Ugh! He Inspects Everything in the Room 3

On Receiving, Back Home in Blighty,
    a Postcard from an Exponent of Free Love 4

Tepid Honeymoon on the Broads 5

The Impossible Dream 5

Back from the Wars 6

Saturday, 3rd August, 2013 6

In the Flesh 7

Over and Under the Tablecloth at Fortnum's 7

Paedophiliac Bee 8

Snobbish Diary Notes After Sex with Hotel Porter 8

Animality 8

Thoughts During Post-Opera Supper 9

Happiness 10

To be Perfectly Candid, Darling   11

Insatiability   12

With a Gracious Publican in his Taproom
     during a Lock-In   12

On Taking Angiotension Converting
     Enzyme Tablets   13

Hieland Laddies   13

White Student Questions Black Professor
     During Tutorial   14

Recommendation on Channel 4 by Percival Twee   14

Spoken in Confidence to a Stranger on a Train   15

Sorry, Dad, I'm Shopping You   16

Withering Rejections   17

Drunk on a Summer's Night   18

Injustice   19

Amarcord   19

Audition   20

Purchased Admiration   20

Courting a Muslim   21

Agreed Starter   22

Tit for Tat   22

Quintet   23

When Penetrated for the First Time   24

Suck it and See   25

Oliver Pater   26

Courtesy   26

My Turn   27

Apologia for Jimmy Savile   27

Lights-Out Patrol   28

The Glutton   28

Financial Independence   28

Mr Lucky   29

Mathematician's Request   29

Repressed Day Dog   29

'July, 2013. Police are Stopping and Searching Too Diligently, According to Home Secretary.' Well, They're not Stopping and Searching Me Ever!   30

Never the Twain   32

Rummaging   33

Oh No! Not Another Scandal in the Groves of Academe   33

Disrespect   34

Stupid Question, Obvious Answer   34

Bitterness   35

Giles, the Candid Host   35

Bus Driver   35

Gardener at Job Interview   36

Little Miss Muffet   36

OAP   37

Versailles   37

Sportsmaster after Nets   37

Mixed Doubles   38

Stuck-Up   39

Breakfast with the Cardinal   39

Equality at Any Cost   39

Sandy   40

Goodbye to all That Exorbitant Expense   40

Two Irishmen and a Bunk Bed   40

Informational Snippet   42

Urgent Message   42

Speedy Conversion   43

The Celibate   44

Half of Big Boy Reg is Quite Enough   45

Strictly for the Birds   45

The Realist   45

Sinner to Too Eager a Confessor   46

Lot   46

The Key to Success   46

Dan of the Heath   47

Sterility be Praised   48

No Logs   48

Lavender Rejection   49

Mutuality   49

Zak's Organ   50

Voluntary Social Worker   50

Safety First   51

Monkish Contentment at Last   51

Scrupulous, Modest, Apologetic Uncle,
    in the Grip of Irresistible Urge,
    Pleads with Unsavoury Nephew   52

Male Chauvinism   53

Drained Cricket Partner   53

"Get this inside you!"   53

Cavemen's Nightlife   54

Frustrated Transsexual Berates Former
    Boyfriend, Not Exactly Enthused
    by Her New Accoutrements   54

Rugby   55

Crime Passionelle   55

Joining the London Library   55

The Back Room   56

Unsympathetic Reaction to Another's Impotency   57

Learning to Tongue   58

Should I, perhaps, not have placed among
    the condiments a little vase with a
    rose therein? And, perhaps, the silver
    (genuine) tray was also a mistake?   58

Saintliness   59

Wilfred   59

Cruising   60

Catty Drag Queen   60

Anchorites   60

There was Only One Gift I Wanted   61

Grayson amd Chris   62

Last Orders   62

Male Twins   63

Toodle Pip   64

Gloom on St. Valentine's Day   64

On Marriage at a Late Age into Poverty
   and Continuous Demands for
   Physical Excitement   65

Beauty and Beast   66

One of the Social Media Christmas Messages
   Sent by 'Two-Way' Teddy Tomkins in 2013   67

First Things First   68

HOMOPHOBIC MAYHEM IN KILBURN   68

A Paedophile Bemoans His Lot   69

Promiscuity

"May I share you?"

"What a question! Of *course!*

How *dare* you!"

Paranoia
or
The Past is Unspeakable in a Police State

"Do you miss it?"

"Be explicit."

"You know: ...."

"That was many, many years ago,

But walls now have ears

To bug elderly queers

So I dare not reply Yes or No."

Housemaster's Pep Talk to Recent Admission

"Now you want it, now you don't,
When all or nothing is our wont.
You must have expected a different school:
Here regularity is the rule –
That's what's meant by a Decent Education,
Not fits and starts, not syncopated
                              dissipation!"

Obdurate Feminist on a Royal Firstborn

"I could have accepted an hermaphrodite,
But a baby *boy* seems hardly fair or right.
Let's hope that, at the least, he will mature
                    into a Ganymedean Heteroclite."

Dinner-Party Spat

"You have the audacity to draw our
attention to the fact you have been
presented with a dirty knife
When my wife and I, out of the kindness
of our hearts, invited you to dine with us
despite your reputedly *unclean life!*"

Ugh! He Inspects Everything
in the Room!

"Is it the hallmark of good breeding to
examine my ornaments, my furniture
with such interested intensity?
After all, I invited you here only for
depravity,
And I'll be paying you afterwards
not a Household Valuation Fee but for
your physical prowess and your
sexual dexterity."

On Receiving, Back Home in Blighty, a Postcard from an Exponent of Free Love

"Little to tell

Save we're both well

On my mentoring spell.

Will give you a bell

When we reach La Rochelle.

Playing lots of Jacques Brel.

I do miss your smell."

As I miss yours,

And I'm hurting like hell.

Tepid Honeymoon on the Broads

"It's been a week now. How have you
               found it, Phil?"
"More 'live and let live' than addictive. Still,
Two ageing chronic boozers can't be
               choosers, can we, Bill?,
And, though not in love, at least we
               haven't fallen in the swill."

The Impossible Dream

"If Boris*
Were the same as Maurice**,
I'd have a shot,
But he is not."

* The Mayor of London.
** Homosexual gamekeeper and eponymous hero of
the novel by E.M.Forster.

5

Back from the Wars

Slow to undress –

Combat stress.

Nevertheless...

Saturday, 3rd August, 2013

Today begins the Football Season.

How many follow it for a homo-erotic

reason?

I'm sure, however, that none of the

players, straight or not yet out,

Resents the Pink Ticket's monetary clout.

In the Flesh

"I'm suffering from a penile dysfunction.
Let's, alternatively, have luncheon."
And it proved more agreeable, together
                                    not alone,
Each of them afterwards felt bound to
                                    own,
Than their customary routine of sex over
                                    the phone.

Over and Under the Tablecloth at Fortnum's

"This is a 'for-God's-sake-turn-off-your-
                                    mobile' plea:
I really would prefer you talked to *me*!
You did, remember?, invite me here to tea.
Your manners are disappointing, Zebedee.
Not that I object to your other hand,
                                    roaming so free."

Paedophiliac Bee

"I hope you're doing this because you
love me, sonny,
And it isn't just you want the honey."

Snobbish Diary Notes after Sex with Hotel Doorman

Body : hunky.
Performance : clunky.
Avoid a flunkey.

Animality

"Are you disturbed by the rough
treatment some animals are getting?"
"Not a bit. I myself have always been
seriously into heavy petting."

Thoughts During Post-Opera Supper

The Garden, The Caprice...all these frills
In order to be polite, to be civilised before
the thrills,
When all we desire is to let go *at once*, to
roll in the mud, wallow.
Don't such diversions seem somewhat
hollow?
The suspense is killing for both of us,
without sense.
In addition for you, there's the devilish
expense.

Happiness

I call him Liquorice Allsorts.
He dresses in many a hue.
His parts are of differing sizes.
We met on a platform at Crewe.

I chew him every morning.
He chews me every night.
I go to work all smiley.
I get my share all right.

He calls me Sugar Candy.
We sometimes coalesce.
I'm sweet and full of brandy.
It's better than Eton Mess.

Neither of us is jealous.
When we give ourselves away
At Christmas and on birthdays,
There isn't hell to pay.

Life is for giving, sharing,

Not sometimes, all the time.

What pleasure to be a poet,

To have turned this tasteful rhyme.

To be Perfectly Candid, Darling

"I'm doing this beyond my norm.

You're merely a fag hag in a storm.

I'm lonely, rejected by a present *beau*;

I'm a two-faced cad, a gigolo,

Contemptible, a kind of thief;

I'm only assuaging a temporary grief."

Insatiability

"Sorry, Freddie,

I'm over-sexed.

Next!

And the next get ready!"

With a Gracious Publican in his Taproom during a Lock-In

"You give such generous measure!

How you enhance my leisure!

You're a treasure!"

"My pleasure!"

On Taking Angiotension Converting Enzyme Tablets

"What is your reaction to seeing from the

rear row upon row of Muslims

at prayer?"

"An accelerated pulse-rate. On Fridays

I go spare."

Hieland Laddies

The Scots wear skirts of tartan plaid,

Concealing priceless treasure.

Have your fling. Dance your measure.

Sing to the laird. Be glad.

White Student Questions Black Professor During Tutorial

"Is it true that most Africans are
    remarkably well-endowed, Dr O'Mara?"
"Off the cuff I'd say Yes – ahem –
    particularly South of the Sahara!"

Recommendation on Channel 4 by Percival Twee

"Actually I've discovered making the
                ultimate sacrifice
Is in no way iffy, but really rather nice.
He'd a small cock so it was all over in a
                trice,
And he was wearig the loveliest of male
    fragrances: Old Spice."

Spoken in Confidence to a Stranger on a Train

"Unable last week to keep the peace
   with my uncivil *premier danseur* partner,
I went out into the streets to find release.
Imagine my surprise at discovering, after
                several hours, my legal mate
In the embrace of a nightwatchman in
                Emperor's Gate.
However, truth to tell, we made a very
                satisfactory Civil Triumvirate –
Nightwatchman, rhymester, famous
                dancer –
And I have come to the conclusion that to
                mend it never is too late,
That, for me at least, troilism has proved
                to be the answer."

Sorry, Dad, I'm Shopping You

"You haven't always behaved proper.
I'm intending, therefore, to inform
                              a copper.
You lifted me - behaviour rudely rum –
When we went paddling at Whitby, and
                    kissed me on my naked bum.
I realise that it was long ago – forty years,
                    in fact, in *chronological* time, –
But the repugnant memory has
                    remained inside my head
                              like psychological slime.
You are undoubtedly, retrospectively and
                    contemporaneously, incestually
                                        bent.
Shame on you! How, at the age of three
         and three quarters, even were this a
              defence, could I have given you
                         my filial consent?!
You committed, within Society's Code of
    Purity, an historic crime for which,
              by full vigour of the Law, you must
              be made to cleanse and heal your
                   rottenness and then repent!"

Withering Rejections

1.

To be frank, I practise fully on less puny

males.

You'll do, though, as my keyboard for

some introductory scales."

2.

The experience has – how can I put it? –

left my boots a little muddy.

Before entering into a relationship, I'd

need, including of course as a *sine qua non*

all Health and Safety matters, a

comprehensive Feasibility Study."

3.

"Sorry to be unresponsive. Firstly, you're
not, by a very long chalk indeed, my
priapic type.
Secondly, and no less importantly, you
talk nothing but unmitigated
drivel, i.e., where I come from,
intellectually specious tripe."

Drunk on a Summer's Night

We are dishes, and we sit and we spoon
Here on this tree-trunk under the moon.
A dog and a cat and a cow we see,
And each of them is as happy as we.

Injustice

Womenfolk show straps and bras
By wearing see-through blouses.
Why can't men be kinky too
With pants in see-through trouse(r)s?

Amarcord

I met a peacock in the snow.
His tail was far from weeny.
"It once was in a film!" he cried.
"It even thrilled Fellini."

Audition
or
Spring Surge of Brighton Choirmaster

"I *adore* a treble that doesn't screech!

Be a pebble on my beach!"

Purchased Admiration

Some judge a fellow by his friends

Of which he hadn't many:

Some by his branded underwear –

This cost him a pretty penny.

Courting a Muslim

1.

Born Again Christian Courts a Muslim

"I'd awfully like to be your pal.
I'd do the very best I can,
Toeing the line at Ramadan.
But is it a problem that I'm not halal?"

2.

Gay 'Fatty' Ali Holds a Secret

'The next Mohammed will be born

                                    of a man'
He believes is implied in the Holy Qu'ran*
And he's helping out as best he can.
When anti-fats taunt, " Expecting a baby?",
He replies with a po-faced and circumspect,
                                    "Maybe."

* 'Qu'ran' to be pronounced with a short 'a'

Agreed Starter

"To me, your knob

Is like corn on the cob.

Please may I nibble?"

"Why yes! I shan't quibble!

No prob!"

Tit for Tat
or
Young Fashion

"Why won't you hold my hand in the street?!

I'm *sick* of your being so bloody discreet!"

"Because you flaunt underpants down to

the thigh

With GOK* on the arse. I'm ashamed!

I'm could die!"

*Gok Wan. A fashion guru of considerable influence
on women and gay men.

Quintet

1.

Wish I wasn't charming.
I'm pulled from left to right.
Men and women, children –
They all must have a bite.

2.

Wish I wasn't handsome.
It makes me look a toff.
The plebs won't risk rejection:
They think I'll say, "Fuck off!"

3.

Wish I wasn't cuddly.
I'm hugged till I feel sick.
And, when you're just a pillow,
Who'll activate your dick?

4.

Wish I wasn't cheesecake,

A muscle-bar, a dream.

What regular chap would pay my flight

To Hollywood from Cheam?

5.

Wish I was cuddly, charming,

Cheesecake, handsome, more...

Everything in one for Jim,

The golden boy next door.

When Penetrated for the First Time

"Do you feel fulfilled at last, Joe?"

"Only moderately so.

Here's an extension. Have another go."

Suck It and See

His mother made him suck her tits
And then gave him a dummy,
So now he cannot help himself –
He sucks our dicks for money.
They say he's pleasured royalty;
I've seen him down on sailors;
When put inside for public wrong,
It's said he sucked his gaolers.
I'd use him oftener I would,
If I wasn't apprehensive
Of, you know, HIV and things
And his being so expensive.
I agree, though, he's a service
That should be NHS.
He deserves a bloody gong he does
For alleviating stress.
I work in dull Insurance.
His good fortune drives me wild,
And it's all because his mother
Stopped him squawking as a child.

Oliver Pater

I never eat out now with Oliver Pater.

He eyes other diners, flirts with the waiter.

He's what you might call a

                'dining-out-traitor',

Easy in public, best in bed later.

Courtesy

"You propose to poke me although I am a

                bloke?!"

"Yes. May I your tolerance invoke?

I've thought about this long and hard,

And my lust your bodily components

                stoke."

"This once, then. First don a condom –

                I daren't my safety disregard.

Then go, stand naked by the tap in the

                back yard."

My Turn

"Pass, old chap,

The controlling strap.

Tonight, *I* reign

And it's *you* who shall complain

In vain."

Apologia for Jimmy Savile
or
Not Everyone was Afeared

"He hugged and kissed and fondled me –

Sometimes all the three.

Let no one accuse him haphazardly

   of discriminate wantoness, of insobriety.

He heard my plea,

Showed me charity,

R.I.P."

Lights-Out Patrol

Comforts (creature).
Downfall (teacher).

The Glutton

"Is it true he's into beating?"
"Yes. He even smacks his lips when

eating."

Financial Independence

Wanky, wanky,
Wank, wank, wank.
Drawing on our private bank.
We only have ourselves to thank.
Wanky, wanky,
Wank, wank, wank.

Mr Lucky

"I'm overkissed.
Desist!"

Mathematician's Request

"Try not to come too soon –
            I see you're already enlargin'.
Take your time, show, as it were,
           all working out in the margin."

Repressed Day Dog (Gay)

His mother dropped him at the school
      each day in envelopes marked
           'DO NOT BEND'.
No wonder his sexual beginnings
      were of a Russian blend.

'July, 2013. Police are Stopping and Searching Too Diligently, According to Home Secretary.' Well, They're not Stopping and Searching <u>Me</u> <u>Ever</u>!

Put your hands inside my pockets,
Run them down my legs.
Can't you see I am a danger?
Can't you see that I'm the dregs?

Why, though, when I scowl and fidget,
Why, though, when I spit and swear,
Do I not appear suspicious,
To you who stand inactive there?

Search me, *search,* I beg of you,
You guardians of this city!
I won't complain if you are rough,
Especially if you're pretty.

Night after night, day after day,
I strike a guilty pose
To get your bobby-mitts on me.
Must I remove my clothes?

Move please to Administration,
Dismount from your high horse!
I'd stand a better tactile chance
With *keen* men in the force.

Meanwhile, till there's greater ardour,
You lackadaisical *beaux gendarmes*,
Your blindness, deliberate, is goading me –
A boy in blue could come to harm.

Weren't you trained to do your duty,
Not be casual, weak, inept?
Police are paid not to be goofy.
Standards, rules are to be kept.

Tonight, trolling with a hunting-knife,

Over one shoulder a bag of hay,

I seek some heavy how's-your-father,

None of your looking the other way.

Gird your loins and roll me gladly!

Raddle me with a taser ray!

Abstain from working your beat so badly!

Ignore the qualms of Tessa May*!

*The Rt. Hon. Theresa May MP, Secretary of State for
the Home Department.

Never the Twain

"Thank you for the gargantuan feast.

Let me give you £80 at the least."

"The very least! This is the West End, not

the East!"

Rummaging

"Oh dear!

What have we here?!"

Oh No! Not Another Scandal in the Groves of Academe
or
Should I Withdraw My Son from such a Topnotch School?

"Sometimes we go, Dad, to the fountain to
drink."

"The fountain?" "Well, what do you
think?!

Our Fountain of Knowledge,

The Head of the College,

Our Physical Mentor, wink, wink."

Disrespect

"He called me a Jock and a seminal

spittoon,

So now he rests at the bottom of Loch

Doon."

Stupid Question, Obvious Answer

"Why do you consider sporting a mirror

on a stick, when holidaying

in Scotland, a veritable duty?"

"I mean to discover areas of outstanding

natural beauty."

Bitterness

"Why can't 'gay' just mean 'happy',
Mummy?"
"The best person to ask is your Father,
dummy."

Giles, the Candid Host

"You'll be receiving today as per usual,
Giles?"
"Alas it's a No. A severe case of piles –
Fault probably yours but it could have
been Myles'."

Bus Driver

"Are you perverted?"
"Shall we say I like to be diverted?"

Gardener at Job Interview

"Gardenin' isn't just the weedin'.

Put a tool in me 'and

And

I'll create you an Eden."

Little Miss Muffet

Little Miss Muffet,

Who sat on that tuffet,

Was really a man in disguise

And a hot reprobate,

But the spider was straight

And ran from the scene in surprise.

OAP

"So what have you been up to then?"
"It's more *down* to, and *that's*
Only granted me now and again."

Versailles

"*Must* you splash so much of that
                              perfume on?!"
"Yes, to defend myself against your
                              stench, *cochon!*"

Sportsmaster after Nets

"I gave you an hour of legspinners,
                              young Ross.
I need now from *you* a 'Sir, thank you
                              full- toss'."

Mixed Doubles

"I'm feeling electric.
I'm hard as a rock.
Lie on your front
And you'll get a nice shock."

"I'm not so eclectic.
To me that's shock horror.
I want your wife's cunt,
And at once, not tomorrow."

"I've just had *your* wife
Up the rear. No complaint.
You think it's shock horror.
She didn't. It ain't."

"All right, then. I'll let you.
It can't be a sin.
First pass me the Gordon's,
And don't stay long in."

Stuck-Up

"I wish you wouldn't call me 'mate'.
Mates we'll never be.
You're rather common, I can tell.
You're Radio 2, I'm 3."

Equality at Any Cost

Promise not to laugh!
They split when one described the other
                              as his 'better half'.

Breakfast with the Cardinal

"Masturbate on your kipper plate –
That is if you have to, mate!
But promise not to pontificate!"

Sandy

Sandy's always rushing,
He hasn't time to talk,
And so I cannot tell him
He has a silly walk.

Sandy's always rushing,
He hasn't time to speak,
And so I cannot tell him
He's known as Sandy Freak.

Sandy's always rushing.
I *could* shout, "Stop! Attention!"
To demean myself, however,
Is far from my intention.

I long to kiss his rosy lips,
Become his long-term lover.
His rushing past is agony.
I doubt if I'll recover.

Goodbye to all That Exorbitant Expense

"Money, money, money! You're always

wanting more!

I thought our love was free, you whore!

You're free to use that door!"

Two Irishmen and a Bunk Bed

"Will ye make love? I feel left on the

shelf."

"Come ye right down and climb up on

meshelf!"

Informational Snippet

Here's a thing to mark and learn:
Rosencrantz and Guildenstern
Wore one another's cods in turn.

Urgent Message

"Put myself in party mood:
Drank far more than I really should.
At present in bed with an East End hood,
Still pissed as a newt, and three times
                                    screwed.
Don't adopt a high moral tone,
Just come and collect. Address unknown."

Speedy Conversion

I took a boy home name of Roddy.
I asked if he'd like a hot toddy.
He looked at me wryly,
Come to think, it was slyly,
And said, "What I want is your body."

I reacted with "You've got a nerve!
I was not put on Earth *boys* to serve.
I'm cut to the quick.
Leave at once. You are sick.
I'm old and you're young. You're a perv."

He looked at me straight in the eye,
Said, "You're stupid and narrow and shy.
You don't know what you're missing!"
And he then began kissing
Me, partly undoing my tie

I've never felt such a revulsion

Yet soon, in a sobbing convulsion,

I begged from the floor, "Stay the night

I implore!

I'm a pederast now by compulsion."

A pity, of altered presuasion,

I only can rise on occasion.

Where the sun doesn't shine

The lad rarely is mine.

I'm his, though, and welcome invasion.

The Celibate

He longed to have a stopcock to stop him

no, not screwing...

His laundry bill was massive:

wet dreams were his undoing.

Half of Big Boy Reg is Quite Enough

"No. Only undress from waist down, my

dear Reg.

I simply require, as vulgarians say,

your meat and two veg.

Strictly for the Birds

Don't, men, waste your time on Lance.

He'll lead you a most unmerry dance:

You won't stand even a spurting chance.

The Realist

"Love's too precious to expend.

Let's settle for some lust, my friend."

Sinner to Too Eager a Confessor

"'Contrition'! 'Absolution'! 'Grace'!
Have a heart! Don't force the pace!"

Lot

"Since the wife turned to salt, I've liked
                    males in the sack,
And, excepting my daughters, *I* haven't
                    looked back."

The Key to Success

His voice is a corncrake's.
He sweats like a pig.
How did he get there?
His bone's ultra big.

Dan of the Heath

This happened in late last October.
In the back of his van
He kissed me, did Dan,
And for once in his life he was sober.

Catch as catch can,
With glimmering hope
I risked, "Don't ever tope,
Be my bitch and I'll stay as your man."

He roared, "*And* leave off dope,
I suppose!! NO, I'M DAN!!!"
And he grabbed at a rope,
I jumped out of that van
And I ran.

Sterility be Praised

A Paddy called Blankety Blank
Is minus all sperm in his tank.
Most world population
Will die of starvation.
Those left will know whom they should

thank.

No Logs

A man in a Chelsea Men's bog
Is known for not dropping a log,
Yet he sits there for hours
Holding sweet scented flowers
In the hope that the drain he will clog.

Lavender Rejection

I met a *garçon* once in Grasse.

I asked him to lend me his ass.

"I *don't* do *comme ça,* give such

ooh-la-la-la!"

He cried. Clearly we'd reached an *impasse*.

Mutuality

A lad in a carpentry store

Returned the mad lust of a door.

He banged it like hell

Till, unhinged, the thing fell

To the floor where it asked him for more.

Zak's Organ

There was a young fellow called Zak

Whose organ was long as his back.

I asked his best mate

What in bed was his fate.

He replied, "I can't take, so I frack."

Voluntary Social Worker

There was kind man from Thamesmead.

He'd a need to teach prisoners to read –

Or thought that he had

Till he went to the bad.

He'll be blind by the time he is freed.

Safety First

My Boss takes his money, not light,

To the bank in his pants, out of sight.

They are made of stretch-nylon

And look simply vile on.

A shame that security's tight.

Monkish Contentment at Last

The she-she of most conversation

For James was a deep irritation.

But no mental disorder

When he entered an order!

He-he won his full approbation.

Scrupulous, Modest, Apologetic Uncle, in the Grip of Irresistible Urge, Pleads with Unsavoury Nephew

"I'm sure you do not care for me one whit,
and I do not wish to compromise your
masculinity. It is not *your* actions that
will be the most revealing,
It will be *my* strength of feeling:
It is to your kindness and to your good
manners that I am appealing.
Undress, dear boy! Let me enfold you!
Hear how I beg! Look!
I bend the knee, and it is *you*
to whom I'm kneeling!"
"Oh, don't make such a fuss, old fool!
Can't you tell I'm gagging for it,
squealing?!!"

Male Chauvinism

"Though my name is Evelyn Hilary
Claude,
I'm a nulliparous man, thank the Lord."

Drained Cricket Partner

(Yawning) : "*Again* he's getting off his rocks!
Does he *ever* think outside of what I have
inside my box?!"

"Get <u>this</u> inside you!"

Thought he'd been offered a piece of cake.
Discovered he'd made an unfortunate
mistake.

Cavemen's Nightlife

On Saturdays
Went clubbing . . . gays.

Frustrated Transsexual Berates Former Boyfriend, Not Exactly Enthused by Her New Accoutrements

"Oh stop your quibbling!
Squeeze these, and remember that the new
frontal space inside me was made
especially for your dibbling!"

Rugby

Another ruck:
Another fuck.

Crime Passionelle

"Lousy in bed.
'Fraid I saw red."

Joining the London Library

"May one relax
Among the stacks?"
He asked the poker-faced Librarian.
"And, nudge, nudge, I'm not referring to
                              anything agrarian!"

The Back Room

Off with our trousers,
Down with our drawers,
Here in the Back Room
In twos, threes and fours.

We suffer our day jobs
For pleasures like this,
Not seeing the faces
Attached to each kiss.

Whom do we savour,
In whom take delight?
We've hardly a clue;
We're moles digging night.

That we're sinful is bosh.
We do nothing Hieronymus.
We're holy in darkness.
We're saintly anonymous.

No one is spurned.

We no one despise.

To all we are kindly,

Regardless of size –

These last words are specious.

I must honestly say

Our hormones need honkers*:

If you're small, stay away.

*Given the propensity of most homosexuals to prefer large penises to play with, the less well-endowed, if they patronised The Back Room, would not stand a chance of more than occasional attention.

Unsympathetic Reaction to Another's Impotency

"What's up? Or should I say 'not up'? You
don't seem to be juiced."
"I'm afraid I'm in need of a Viagra boost."
"And to think you were once our cock of
the walk, ruled our roost!"

Learning to Tongue

"I said 'rear' not 'ear'.

No. Do not recoil!

Though dashing my hopes,

You're on the nursery slopes

And I won't your evening spoil."

Should I, perhaps, not have placed among the condiments a little vase with a rose therein? And, perhaps, the silver (genuine) tray was also a mistake?

I took breakfast-in-bed to him on a silver

tray,

Then lunch.

I have a hunch.

He thinks he's here to stay.

Saintliness

There's this hetero I know, and I love him
                                                    fit to bust.
Though male-exempted,
Never tempted,
He gives generously to London Lighthouse
                        and the Terrence Higgins Trust*.

*Charities which help homosexuals.

Wilfred

"Is he gay?"
"No, grey:
Gay every other day –
Except, of course, when he's drunk.
            Then he'll do anything any old way."

Cruising

"People talk to me of specifically gay

pick-up joints.

I myself have always found that *nowhere*

disappoints."

Catty Drag Queen

Stiff as a poker,

I feared I would choke her.

But she leapt out of bed,

Wig still on her head,

"Your *fleas* could do better," she said.

Anchorites

"Would an anchorite?"

"Approached too soon, he'd fight.

After time, though, I think he might."

There was Only One Gift I Wanted

He gave me cheese; he gave me port;

He gave me chocs, the sod. He

Can't have guessed they'd be chucked in

                                        my bin

With his dog-in-the-manger body.

Grayson and Chris

"What's your preference, Chris?"

"Anything in trousers – tother ,

                        that and this."

"May I therefore suggest you give

                Grayson Perry* a miss?"

*A transvestite and a potter.

Last Orders

Know your Classical Greek?
It is *young men* I seek
Of whose love I dare speak,
And I want them at once and not then.

No, I *don't* want a girl
I want cocks that unfurl,
The big balls of a churl,
So promise you won't bring a hen.

Spread the word fast
As I've not long to last.
Add I like them plump-arsed
For fucking again and again.

Burgle each bedroom,
Say I also give headroom.
Quick! There's no time to sex-groom.
I'm almost a hundred and ten.

Male Twins

"The older I become, my sexual desires
                   in range and intensity increase.
I'd hoped in the autumnal years to find
                   some blessed peace."

"I envy you. I'd anticipated playing new,
      exciting tunes on this my poor old fiddle,
But all I'm ever left with are pressing urges
                   to have another Jimmy Riddle."

"Isn't talk of Jimmy Riddle rather crude
                   within a pome?"
"You literary snob! Take your filthy
                   paws off me! I'm going home!"

Toodle Pip

I know a man called Toodle Pip.

For years I've sought his comradeship.

But, just when I've undone his zip,

He disappears, gives me the slip.

I want, too, to talk about Loyola,

William Faulkner, Emile Zola...,

But, just when I've accessed his brain,

He steals away from where we're lain.

Must this continue till I die?

What else – his *soul*? – is left to try?

And, if this also fails, to him I'll sigh,

"Toodle pip to you. *Goodbye!*"

Gloom on St. Valentine's Day

Bang! Bang! My heart is full of lead.

I'm dead.

On Marriage at a Late Age into Poverty and Continuous Demands for Physical Excitement

Chrysanths are the poor man's flowers,

Tinned baked beans are his food;

These, and you into the bargain,

I'm finding too harsh, too crude.

McDonald's is our eating out

And oil our heating in;

These, and having you as well,

I cease to bear and grin.

Gone are my hopes of yesteryear:

A bugger can't be chooser.

But it's giving you my sperm non-stop

Most turns me into loser.

Demands to ride your greedy back,

Here and there, wherever,

Inside the sack, outside the sack –

This can't go on forever.

My juices drain, my powers wane:

I'm getting out of breath.

I must deny your passive lust

Or face an early death.

Please, soon as poss, place me in a Home,

Find a new 'top' for sharing.

To compensate for my time with you

I need palliative caring.

Beauty and Beast

His face is his fortune as is his secret place,

Or as are such places – I mean no disgrace.

One of the Social Media Christmas Messages Sent by 'Two-Way' Teddy Tomkins in 2013

As you may already know, I've consented
this year to being riven,
So please book early during the busy
Festive Season.
Post-Epiphany, however, I shall be
returning to merely giving,
That is until the Lenten Lull when I'll be
making my usual attempts to end up
shriven,
The results of which – negative or positive –
I intend to disseminate electronically on
he date that Christ Our Lord was risen.

First Things First

"Because I'm in straightened circumstances
                    doesn't mean I'm straight,
As I now intend to demonstrate.
I'm afraid that the mug of tea I offered will
                    have to wait."

HOMOPHOBIC MAYHEM IN KILBURN

"*Landlord,* the filth here hash thickened
                    too bloody far!"
Boomed Paddy the Builder from South
                    Mullingar,
When groped yet again while enjoying a jar*.
"As a practishing papisht I'm raising the
                    bar!"
And raze it he did bannered *Mirror* and *Star.*

* His fourth or fifth.

A Paedophile Bemoans His Lot

Some scout for girls, I scout for boys.

The younger the better. They're toys.

But, oh, life's not easy.

I'm thought to be sleazy.

Whatever I do it annoys.

I can't show affection,

Insert my erection,

Even to show it makes noise.

It's the parents who shout

When sex is about.

Boys, they will always be boys.

I'm trapped in a box,

Caged by parents' faux shocks.

Without them my way could be done;

The weather'd be sunny,

I'd chase each boy bunny,

Run free as a fox, have some fun.